Amazon
Adventures

By Horace Banner

About the Author...

Horace Banner was a pioneer missionary who served with the Unevangelised Field Mission (UFM) Worldwide. He loved the people of the Amazonian Rain Forest and for over 40 years, in obedience to God's call, he gave himself to the Lord's work among the Kayapo people. Called by God to serve among these people in Brazil, Horace and his wife Eva joyfully accepted that commission. They showed remarkable courage, tenacity and love as they became the first missionaries to live among the fierce Kayapos in a tribal village.

Horace and Eva, and later their children, Jessie Mae and James, identified with these people and entered into their culture. They related well to this tribal people and were loved and accepted by them. Horace began the task of reducing the Kayapo language into writing. Later he translated portions of the Bible and wrote hymns which the Kaypo are still singing. Instead of violence, peace became the norm in the area and a number came to know and love the Lord Jesus. To the Kayapo, Horace was a preacher, teacher, healer, brother, friend and helper in many ways. He became a recognised authority on Kayapo culture and was made an honorary citizen of Brazil, receiving a citation and a medal for his outstanding service to that land.

Above everything, Horace was a man who knew and loved God. Unassuming and utterly selfless, he looked upon every problem as a golden opportunity to get closer to his Saviour. His delight was to endeavour to bring others to the Saviour. He longed that others would see something of the Lord's wisdom, love and power in his life. May the Lord of the harvest call many more to follow the example of this godly man and join the mission with which he served for so long!

George P Rabey
UFM Worldwide

'Ask the beasts and they shall teach thee!' wrote the observant Job. Following his wise and ancient advice, Horace and Dona Eva feel they have learned so much from their experiences in the Amazonian Rain Forest, and now in this book, seek to pass on some of the lessons learned.

Look for the other title in this series:
Rain Forest Adventures
ISBN: 1-85792-627-7

Published by Christian Focus Publications Ltd
Geanies House, Tain, Ross-shire, IV20 1TW
© Copyright2001 Christian Focus Publications
Cover Illustration by Graham Kennedy
Allied Artists
All other illustrations by Stuart Mingham
ISBN 1-85792-440-1
www.christianfocus.com
email: info@christianfocus.com
Printed by Guernsey Press, Guernsey, U.K.

To find out more about UFM Worldwide, with whom
Horace Banner was a missionary, please contact:-

UFM Worldwide
47a Fleet Street
Swindon Wiltshire SN1 1RE

Tel: 01793 610515
Fax: 01793 432255

email: ufm@ufm.org.uk

website. www.ufm.org.uk

UFM Worldwide

UFM Worldwide began in 1931 as "The Unevangelised Fields Mission". The mission is committed to taking the Gospel to unreached people around the world.

The first UFM missionaries worked in Brazil and Congo. Today the work involves 85 missionaries working in 16 countries in Africa, Asia, Asia Pacific, Europe and South America.

UFM missionaries are evangelical Christians who have a clear sense of call to missionary service which has been confirmed by their local church.

UFM's priority is to take the Gospel to people who have had least opportunity to hear it. They concentrate particularly on evangelism, church planting and leadership training.

UFM works in partnership with churches believing that churches, not mission agencies, send missionaries. They co-operate with national churches in pioneer evangelism. They work on an interdenominational basis with all who affirm the evangelical faith. They are happy to enable missionaries to go to any country in the world.

You can obtain further information about UFM by writing to their Swindon headquarters or by looking at their website at www.ufm.or.uk.

Contents

If you've read *Rainforest Adventures* you will recognise some of your old friends from that book. Not only do Horace and his wife take us through the Rain Forest once again but they also remind us about some of the animals we met in *Rain Forest Adventures*. Look out for the chamelon, the electric eel, the frog and the tortoise. The tapir gets a mention too along with a few other new and interesting animals. Try your hand at our special new quiz at the end of the book. If you haven't read *Rain Forest Adventures* look for it in the shops - as well as finding out about a peccary, an anteater and possums you will discover the dangerous piranha fish and the boa constrictor!

The current produced by an

electric eel is as much as

500 volts!

The Electric Eel

I t was Sunday morning in the Kayapo village, but instead of Sunday School being as usual, the boys were absent. Waking up very hungry, they decided to go fishing.

They were not far away, but school was over when their canoes arrived. And long before they came in sight, everybody knew that they were not coming empty-handed. When there is no kill, or the catch is a small one, the Kayapo are ashamed and try to sneak into the village without being seen. When the haul is big, they make a lot of noise. That Sunday morning the shouting was so loud the kill might well have been a jaguar!

As the
boys came
scrambling up the
river-bank, they were
really excited. They had
something alive, on the end of a
rope-like creeper. It was an
electric eel!

'Here you are!' one
of the boys said to
me.

'You often asked us to get one alive. Now you can take its picture.'

I had often seen electric eels, but either dead or gliding about in the water. 'Hang it up on that beam!'

It was a tricky operation, but the boys were most careful to keep out of the wriggling creature's way. I noticed that the drag rope was quite dry. Experience has taught the Kayapo the ABC of insulation. After all, their ancestors knew about electric shocks before ours did!

The eel was not a big one, being just four feet in length and the thickness of a man's arm. It could never be taken for a snake, the dark green body had no scales and there was a soft rippling fin stretching along the underside from head to tail. The head was flat, with the tiniest of eyes and a gaping mouth. The drag rope had been poked through the eel's gills.

The boys were quick to notice my interest in their victim. Asked one; 'Are you white-eyed with us for having fished on the God's day?' (White-eyed is one of their ways of saying angry.)

I might have been sad about the neglected Sunday School, but there was no hiding my interest in that electric-eel. 'So this is the electric eel which is dynamo, battery and discharge coil all combined, going about giving powerful shocks to all and sundry!' I mused.

Having read somewhere that the current produced is as much as 500 volts, I went into the house for my volt-meter. Perhaps by earthing the negative contact and touching that rippling fin or tail with the positive one, there might be some kind of response on the dial.

'Don't touch it, it will knock you down!' yelled the boys. 'Let it die first. Then it won't shock anybody any more.'

I was easily convinced. There was nothing else to do but wait for the electric-eel to die. But I was feeling sad and wondering why all that electricity should have to be wasted. I dreamt of what might have been done with those 500 volts if they could have been harnessed and made useful. To think that all the amazing eel had ever produced had just gone in giving shocks, in electrocuting small crabs and minnows and warning bigger fry to keep off! So much potential light, heat and power just squandered!

The dead eel was cut down and handed back to the boys, who, hungrier than ever, prepared themselves and their victim for the feast. I watched very carefully as they did the cutting and slicing, but saw no clue as to the creature's power plant. However the heart was very close to its mouth and I was surprised to see the heart so small for such a long, powerful body.

The Kayapo believe that they become like the things they eat. They eat the howling monkey to be tough and noisy, the jaguar to be fierce, the electric-eel to be vicious. The stronger and wilder they can become, the better their chances of one day becoming a chief. My Kayapo friends would think that you can learn much from the electric eel... how to be wild and fierce. They would say that God made the electric eel to show us how to be wild and fierce. I would say that God has made the electric eel to show us how not to behave!

The tribal people of the jungle have their own ideals. The heroes of their legends were all fierce warriors with super-strength, magic weapons and a skill for killing. How they marvel at the stories the missionaries tell

them of the Lord Jesus, in everything so different from anybody the Kayapo ever heard or dreamed of. No one was ever so mighty. Only Jesus could say: 'All power is given unto me in heaven and in earth'. Yet for all that power, Jesus was so lovely to know.

Jesus healed many people. Many diseases were cured by his power. His power also calmed waves, cast out demons and even raised the dead. In him all-power was mingled with all-love.

Jesus wants us to be his disciples, to learn of him. We can never be like him by ourselves. Our human nature is so proud, so selfish and unkind. The looks we give, the words we say and the things we do, when thoughtless and unkind, can hurt so much.

When electrical equipment is working properly, there are no shocks, nor is there any wastage. If light is required, it is enough to switch-on, if heat or power, to plug-in. If our actions, looks and words give 'shocks', it is because there is something wrong, something within us, which needs putting right.

The Lord Jesus wants to do just that, and then to make us something which by nature we could never be. He wants to make us like himself. For him to begin working, there is a step which we must take. It is to accept him as our Saviour and Master. As we do this, the Holy Spirit comes into out hearts and with him, something of God's own Life and Light, Love and Power.

What a wonderful thing it is to know the Lord Jesus, to believe in him and to know that he is working in us and through us. Whatever he gives to us and does for us, is for us to pass on, not to keep for ourselves. The world is full of needy people, the sad, the lonely, the disappointed, the sinful. Jesus wants to meet their need, through us.

The Brazilian jungle boasts

some 30,000

different kinds of butterflies.

The White Mayflies

Early one morning, when I opened the door and looked out, I could hardly believe my eyes. There was a long trail of white smoke about 15 feet above the water, as far as the eye could see, both upstream and down. The smoke trail was quite unbroken and it seemed to hover in the air like sky-writing.

Going down the bank to investigate, I discovered that the 'smoke' was alive, not hovering, but moving upstream, made up of millions of tiny butterfly-like creatures flying in close formation.

'Where are they all coming from?' I wondered. 'Surely not from the mouth of the river, so far away? And where are they making for, so early and so eagerly? Surely they do not hope to reach the sources of the river on such flimsy wings?' On and on surged the vast procession, not one of the little creatures straying to either right hand or left. By this time the sun was beginning to peep through the tree tops.

The Brazilian jungle boasts some 30,000 different kinds of butterfly, however these little creatures though very like butterflies were probably more like what you and I would call Mayflies. The sun cast a glimmer of golden light on every busy wing. It was a wonderful sight.

Then down the river bank came a Kayapo tribes-man, carrying his bow and a couple of arrows. *'Zane kuem pa'*, he said. That is the Kayapo way of saying 'Good morning' though literally it means 'The morning is ours'.

The tribes-man was going fishing and was in a hurry. He began to untie one of the canoes moored there in the village 'port'.

I pointed towards the wonderful sight and asked him if he had seen them for himself. He gave a grunt by way of assent. The Kayapo have no word for 'Yes'.
'And where are they all coming from?'
'From the water!' came the brief reply.
'And where are they all going to?'
'To the water,' he grunted as he pushed the canoe into the current and paddled away.

From the water, to the water! Here was a mystery indeed that I must sort out. The sun was now looking right over the trees and the air was warming up.
Suddenly, a single little insect broke rank and lost height. It made frantic efforts to keep going, but after a moment or two, fell into the water and was swept away. As the sun mounted higher in the sky, other tiny wings grew tired, faltered and failed. White wings began to go down by the hundred, the thousand.
From the water, to the water! I could see it now. I wanted to call out to the hundreds and thousands of little creatures which still surged along, quite indifferent to the other casualties.

'Turn aside, turn aside! Can't you see that your turn is coming? Your wings are just as flimsy as those which have already fallen. There is good, solid ground on either bank of the river, and within easy reach. Why don't you turn aside and be safe?'

But they did not because they were created by God with beauty and instinct... and not with the ability to listen or to understand me. On and on they went, busy and eager to the last flutter of their wings, until destruction had overwhelmed every one of them.

From the water, to the water, with a short four-hour life cycle in between!

The morning was still young when the last of the procession had disappeared. The air was left quite clear and even the surface of the water bore no trace of the countless millions it had engulfed. What a parable of the millions of human souls who are today living in time but who will all soon go to eternity.

The Lord Jesus was always moved with compassion as He saw the multitudes go by. He saw them as sheep not having a shepherd. He saw them as in the broad way of sin and self, disobedience and don't care. Hear His warning: Broad is the way that leadeth to Destruction, and many there be which go in thereat' (Matthew 7:13).

It was to save us from that destruction that Jesus came to earth from heaven, to live and die and rise again. 'God so loved the world that He gave His only-begotten Son that whosoever believeth in Him should not perish, but have everlasting life' (John 3:16).

The grasshopper is a member of
the locust family, and locusts
won't leave a plant or tree until
they have stripped it
of every last bit of green.

The Grass-hopper Mind

What is that? My wife Dona Eva was pointing to a big green insect perched on the mosquito-net. It was bed-time, and we were both wanting to get that net between us and the vicious mosquitoes which had been droning around since sundown. And now Dona had discovered a suspicious-looking insect, seated on the net as if just waiting for the light to be blown out. Then, no doubt, he would get to work with his teeth and gnaw his way through the netting, leaving a big hole so that all the hungry mosquitoes could get at us! Shining a light, I saw that it was nothing more than a big variety of grasshopper.

'Nothing to be afraid of,' I called. It's just a grasshopper looking round for some green stuff.'

'That may be true,' replied Dona Eva. 'But do put him out of our bedroom. There's no grass in here.'

So I gave the net a good shake, just like I often did to rid the net of bits of straw blown down from the thatched roof.

The grasshopper was quite unmoved by the shaking. I then gave him a flick, as if he were a wasp or fly. The grasshopper never budged. Finding an old magazine, I rolled it up and gave him a hearty swipe. But never an inch did the intruder retreat.

Finally, very determined, I seized him between thumb and forefinger, and pulled. Even then, he was most reluctant to let go. I noticed that the grasshopper wasn't just holding on with his feet, but with both legs, from the knee downwards. Those legs were fitted with grips like the teeth of a saw, not for cutting, but for holding on.

Seeing himself overpowered, the grasshopper hopped, and a real good hop it was. I went after him to make him hop right out of the house. Imagine my surprise to find him waiting for me, like a boxer coming in for another round! Far from waiting to be shoved outside, he was already turned right round and facing whatever might be coming. But shoved he was, so again he hopped, but making another turn in mid-air, so that when he landed, he was facing the foe.

'Grasshopper, you're game, and no mistake', I muttered. 'Your motto seems to be: *Only give way when you have to, and even then, keep your face to the enemy.*'

Then I thought of other people that I had read of in books and magazines who had 'grasshopper minds'. For instance, there's the person who won't concentrate, who nibbles at everything and masters nothing. There's the boy who hankers for something until he gets it, and then tires of it from one day to another.

There's the girl who, when she should be doing her arithmetic lesson is planning how to spend her pocket money. It is supposed to be the 'grasshopper mind' which keeps these good folks from getting to the top of the form, or any other good place in life.

We all know such people, and they are not all boys and girls at school, by any means. There are lots of them to be found in church! No one can ever tell when they are going to come, or when they will go elsewhere. It is not just their attendance which is casual, either. Their interest is the same. They can listen to the most solemn, challenging message from God's Word, and remain untouched. The moment the 'Amen' is sounded, they begin to talk about the most trivial things. Is that an example of a 'grasshopper' mind? Grasshoppers do hop, of course they do, but not like silly humans! If we see a grasshopper hopping around of his own free will, it is because he is looking for something. He will hop around until he finds it. Then he stays put. He plants his feet and those non-skid legs of his, and there is no moving him until he is through.

The grasshopper is a member of the locust family, and locusts won't leave a plant or tree until they have stripped it of every last bit of green. Locusts are successful because their unity is their strength. The grasshopper's strength is that when he finds what he wants he stays there. Sometimes someone decides to become a Christian but some time later they give up. When temptations come they just can't stand it. Instead of going forward in their Christian life they go backwards. However with a grass-hopper it's different. Its direction is forward, not backward. We may hit him, beat him, knock him down or chase him out, but he's tough. When he moves, it is forward. He's game. When he comes up again, it is facing the enemy.

There was a time when great multitudes followed the Lord Jesus because He had fed them with loaves and fishes. When He spoke to them in His teaching of Living Bread and of Eternal Life, the crowds disappeared. We read that many went back and walked no more with Him (John 6:66-69) Turning to His disciples, Jesus asked whether they would also go. Peter replied for them all.

'Lord, to whom shall we go? Thou hast the words of Eternal Life. And we believe and are sure that Thou art that Christ, the Son of the Living God.' Peter and his friends had been looking for the Messiah for some time before they found him in Jesus. Andrew, for one, had left his nets to go away to Judea where John the Baptist had begun to preach. It was while Andrew was a disciple of John, that Jesus appeared. Andrew was the first to get to know Him. His search was ended. He quickly brought his brother Peter to the Saviour also.

They were not casual Christians. They were not Christians for the sake of the loaves and fishes. They wanted Eternal Life, and having found that in the Lord Jesus, they were His for ever.

'Now I belong to Jesus,
Jesus belongs to me,
Not for the years of
time alone,
But for eternity.'

A chameleon is a reptile

and is therefore cold-blooded.

Any warmth he wants

must come from outside.

That is why he spends so much

time basking in the sun.

The Jungle Turncoat

Journeying by canoe one day, we called a halt for a mid-day meal. After tying up our boat, the Kayapo boy who was with us went scouting around for some dry sticks for the camp fire.

Suddenly, he looked up and after a moment or two pointed to a branch which was overhanging the water.

It was some time before either of us could make out what he was pointing to, but looking very carefully, we could discern a chameleon. Chameleon signifies 'Lion of the Earth'. His picture suggests a relationship with the fierce crocodile. But a chameleon is anything but a fierce creature.

He was holding on to that branch as if his very life depended on it, hugging it tightly with legs and feet and making extra-sure by using his long tail as a hook. How different from the monkeys we see. A monkey, at above sixteen metres (or fifty feet), hangs with superb confidence just by the tip of his tail!

As he lay on that branch, the chameleon was as green as the foliage which almost hid him. At other times, we have seen him grey and spotted. It is said that he is able to change colour at will so as to match his surroundings. That is because he does not want his enemies, and in particular the hawk, to see him.

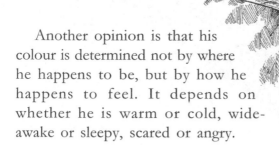

Another opinion is that his colour is determined not by where he happens to be, but by how he happens to feel. It depends on whether he is warm or cold, wide-awake or sleepy, scared or angry.

The poor fellow usually looks very green and feels very cold. I once handled a live chameleon and although the day was a very hot one, the reptile's body was as cold as a dog's muzzle.

All reptiles are cold-blooded. The chameleon is no exception. Any warmth he wants must come from outside. That is why he spends so much time basking in the sun. And as he basks, he dozes. However, this causes a problem should a hawk pounce upon him or a prowling jaguar find him as he sleeps!

Thinking it over, I am very thankful for my own warm blood which keeps steady at 32 degrees centigrade whether I am trekking through steaming jungle or sanding on a cold street corner in a March wind.

How inconvenient it would be if, when we wanted to do a job in the cold, we had to warm up in front of the fire and then rush off to get it done before the heat wore off!

But human beings can be every bit as changeable as chameleons. People use the chameleon as a picture of people who change their opinions as and when it suits them. The chameleon is an animal that people use to describe someone who they can not rely on.

Nobody admires a turncoat. And the variety most despised is the religious one. Who has not met with the person who can look a saintly white on special occasions, but who can change to a shady grey, smutty or even black when the occasion demands? What a hindrance to Christianity are those who profess to be Christians but whose lives are inconsistent!

Peter the apostle was once a turncoat. One night, he made a solemn vow that he would always be faithful to Jesus. Yet before morning, he denied Him three times, pretending that he did not even know who Jesus was.

That evening, in the High Priest's courtyard, Peter stood by a fire to warm himself. But his coldness was such that no fire on earth could deal with. It was spiritual coldness. And Peter was afraid! All the warmth and fervour he had felt when he was with Jesus and the other disciples just disappeared. Peter's whole appearance and bearing changed with his circumstances.

When taunted, the Christian disciple's testimony became the lying and swearing of an ungodly man.

But it only needed one look from the Lord Jesus to bring tears to Peter's eyes and an overwhelming sense of sorrow and shame to his heart. He still believed. He still loved. But he was so weak and unreliable.

Do you ever let Jesus down as Peter did? It's the last thing you want to do. When you are with other Christians you feel so strong and confident. When everything is easy and going well you are so keen and enthusiastic. You are going to keep true to Jesus always, everywhere! Then temptation comes along. You meet with scorn and reproach as Peter did. You feel alone, and your strength and enthusiasm disappear. You find yourself denying your Lord.

To keep keen, constant and true to Jesus, the warmth and strength you get from happy fellowship are not enough. The work of God in you must be personal, real and deep. Prayer and Bible reading are vital for a healthy Christian life. With God's Holy Spirit within you, you will be made strong, kept steady, consistent and dependable, wherever you are and whatever may come.

A single egg from the nest

of an emu or Brazilian ostrich

can weigh just under half a kilo.

The Grand Lady

The way from our village to the outside world is by river. It is best made during the rainy season, when the water is at flood level and travel can be by motor-boat. Summer travel is both difficult and dangerous, for the water is very shallow, the rocks are all uncovered, and the rapids at their worst. But although Dona Eva and I may avoid summer travel, our mail has to come and go, and in the dry months it may take as much as a month to reach the nearest post-office!

Another way to the outside world is by an overland track to the neighbouring Araguaia River, 200 miles away. Half this distance is through uninhabited jungle. Then the trail emerges into a new world of open prairie land. Glad to be free from tangled thickets and falls of timber, the traveller soon misses the forest's cool shade. He may soon be hungry too, for most wild game prefers the shadows to the sun's fierce glare. There are exceptions, of course, and perhaps chief among them is the emu or Brazilian ostrich. A nest of emu eggs is always a great find, for a single egg weighs just under half a kilo or over a pound. How would you like omelette made from ostrich-egg?

The last time we saw the Brazilian ostrich, we were ever so impressed by her stately appearance, her plumes, her long legs and massive body. 'Queen of all Birds!' I reflected. Then I noticed how small her head was, and wondered however it managed to control so much bulk and strength. When we asked the Kayapo what she eats, they smiled and said 'Everything'!

Now, insects and fresh leaves, fruits and berries must be very good for her, for they are brimful of vitamins. But fancy going in for shells, stones, coins and pieces of broken glass!

It seems that for all her great size, she hasn't much common-sense, for she just goes ahead, taking in all that comes, good or bad.

Of course, there are human beings who also 'swallow anything', even believing in lucky horseshoes and black cats and horoscopes and broken mirrors!

Such superstitious beliefs are not for Christians. Believing in Jesus lifts us right above silly superstitions.

However, even Christians need to pray for discernment. The world offers so much that we need to avoid if our faith is to grow and if we are to know and enjoy life at its very best. We must take God's Word as our guide and follow its leading from day to day.

This lack of discernment is not the ostrich's only fault. Whatever are we to think of a bird which does not fly?

Dona Eva says that she would rather be an owl than an ostrich. If she had to be a bird, she would at least expect to fly and be able to by-pass this jungle with its thorns, snakes and jaguars.

But like the rest of us, Dona Eva must live without wings. These bodies of ours are designed and equipped for life on earth.

In every earth-bound body, however, there dwells a spirit which God created and designed for Himself and for Heaven. Many forget this and live as if the earth-life were everything. They have no time or thought for God. They neither praise nor pray.

When Christians pray, they are using their spiritual equipment, their 'wings'. The prophet describes prayer as 'mounting up with wings as eagles'. By waiting upon God, we can rise above all our doubts, fears and problems, and even before we reach the 'Amen', we are all refreshed and strengthened in spirit.

Many young people don't pray because their parents, who used to pray, gave up and never bothered to teach their children the way up to God.

'But the ostrich may not use her wings for flying, but do they not help her to run?'

They do. An ostrich is just about the fastest things on legs. What the ancient Job says about her scorning horse and rider is quite correct (Job 39:18).

From the top of her long periscope neck, she can see danger at more than a mile, and away she goes at a great rate. She only thinks of herself. If there are eggs, or youngsters, she leaves them to take care of themselves, until she gets back. That is, if she can find her way home again, and if someone does not raid the nest while she is away!

Who would want to be raised like a young ostrich, with a selfish, thoughtless mother, for then it would be so easy to grow up unloving, ungrateful and disobedient.

In spite of the ostrich's love of speed and gadding about, she does not usually get very far, for instead of running with her head in command, she only runs with legs and wings. When in danger, if she would only make

for safety and keep a true course, she would be all right, but she will run in great circles. Knowing this, her enemies are waiting for her.

The Kayapo don't confirm about her hiding her head in the sand and thinking that all is well, even when death is right on top of her. But that would be quite in keeping with the rest of her foolish ways.

Queen of all Birds? Not a bit! An ostrich hasn't got sense to match her good looks and great strength, and sense is such an essential qualification for any leader.

What a lesson to us not to let arms and legs and appetites run away with us. We should not waste our gifts nor give our time to getting nowhere.

God has given us head and hearts to control our bodies, and as Christians, we have His Word and the Holy Spirit to guide us and keep even heads and hearts under His direction.

Read what the apostle Paul says about running. He is thinking about the Race of Life.

'Let us lay aside every weight, and the sin which doth so easily beset us, and let us run with patience the race that is set before us. *Looking unto Jesus*, the author and finisher of our faith.' (Hebrews 12:1-2)

A tortoise
can live for
350 years
or more.

A Strange Christmas Dinner

Turkeys, turkeys everywhere, but whoever heard of a Christmas turtle or tortoise?

Here in the Brazilian forest these strange creatures provide us with many a meal. Though there are plenty of wild peccary, roving the forest in mad, snorting herds, it isn't every day that the hunter crosses their trail. But he rarely comes home without a tortoise or two. As for turtles, the river abounds with them. They often take bait meant for fish, and with it, swallow the hook too.

Waiting to go into our pressure cooker is a good-sized tortoise weighing 7 kilos. How sad for him that he should have been picked up by our hunter. Otherwise, he might have gone on eating and growing for two or three centuries! With his shell matching the dead leaves which carpet the forest, he was not easily seen. It was his movement which gave him away.

It seems that the tortoise was never meant to be killed and eaten. With his flat, armour-plate underneath, and the rounded, stream-lined dome on top, he had little to fear from anyone. Rain cannot wet him or hornets sting him. He is safe from both hawks and dogs.

He cannot be crushed by the peccary's hammer-hoofs or the anaconda's coils.

The fierce piranha-fish may snap off a leg as he crosses a river, but such a wound is never fatal. And after being once bitten, he is more than twice shy.

A tortoise was built for long life. It isn't just the defensive armour which helps him. His disposition helps too. He's quiet and easy-going. He makes no enemies.

He never hurries or worries. He makes himself at home anywhere, on land or in the water, in forest, field or back-yard. He never works, for he makes neither burrow nor nest. He isn't bothered with his family. The female just lays her eggs in the sand and lumbers away after something to eat, leaving her eggs for the sand and sun to keep warm and hatch out. The young tortoises never know either of their parents.

The tortoise doesn't envy any of his neighbours. He leaves the armadillo to burrow, the squirrel to hoard his nuts, the parrot to scream, the monkey to frisk about in the tree-tops. He cares about none of these things, but he will be alive for scores of years after his toughest rival is forgotten.

See how he goes, ambling around from tree to tree, hoarding up strength, fat and toughness from the wind-blown wild fruits he doesn't even have to pick.

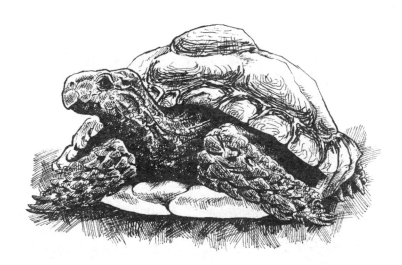

When bad weather comes, he hides and goes to sleep until things get better. When there's danger about, he lies low in his shell until it passes. The only time he exerts himself is when the hunter has him all tied up and he senses that his precious life is in danger. Then he will struggle all night to free himself and get away.

But even tortoises die! Yes, even when for centuries they have eluded the hunter's hatchet or the jaguar's mighty paws. In spite of armour-plate, slow motion and easy going for 350 years or so, they die like anything else! And what have they to show for having lived so long? Just nothing! They never harm anyone, never damage anything. They do nothing but live…and die.

Whoever would want to be a tortoise, even with the 280 years or thereabouts he has over and above the human ration of life?

Methuselah lived much longer than the most ancient tortoise on record. When he passed the 900-year mark, and then 950, he must have felt sure of reaching his thousand. What a time to live! However did he do it? What did he do with so many years? What opportunity to do something really worth while! We read that the days of Methuselah were 969 years, and he died! (Genesis 5:27)

We cannot stay in this world as long as either Methuselah or a Brazilian tortoise, but God does give to most of us a full 70 years of opportunity, not just to live and die, but to do something really worth while in a world so full of human need. He means us to enjoy life to the full by living it for Him and with Him.

The Lord Jesus said: 'He that loveth his life shall lose it'. What a lover of life is the useless old tortoise! And what a picture of so many of us, who for all our intelligence and privilege, are living our lives as vainly and as selfishly as the quaint creature who, after all, is not expected to know any better.

'Whosoever will lose his life for My sake, the same shall find it.' Was the Lord Jesus only speaking of those who die for Him as martyrs? In the New Testament, 'martyr' and 'witness' are translations of the same word! This means that to God, one who lives for Jesus as a 'witness', is just the same as one who dies for Him as a 'martyr'.

I once took one of the tribes-men down to the city to spend some money he earned. Thinking to help the man to make his purchases, I asked: 'Where is your money?'

Imagine my surprise when he replied: 'Oh, I've already lost it all'. Seeing the look of surprise, he repeated: 'Yes, I lost it all, and look what I found'. He then displayed very proudly a shining new knife, a mirror and various articles of clothing.

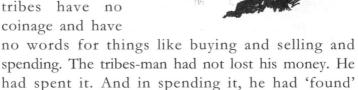

There are no commercial terms in the Kayapo language. The tribes have no coinage and have no words for things like buying and selling and spending. The tribes-man had not lost his money. He had spent it. And in spending it, he had 'found'

something of far more practical value than the few coins he had handed over to the shop-keeper.

So to 'lose' a life for Jesus is surely to 'spend' it for Him, and with Him. How can you do that? First of all, make up your mind that whatever others may or may not be, you are going to be a real Christian and live your life not just for yourself like a tortoise, but for the Lord Jesus who died to make you His own.

Then you can set out to learn something everyday of the week to make you a better disciple. Jesus said: 'Learn of me', and this means more than maths, science and languages. What a lot there is for us to learn as we seek to live for Jesus and be like Him! And that means Life as He meant it to be.

So the tortoise teaches us something as well as making a good sized meal. We Jesus-hearers possess and enjoy something far better than your kind of life. We have life more enduring than that of Methuselah. We know and follow the One who has the words of eternal life.

A tapir's skin is thick and tough so that he is quite indifferent to thorns and stings, and even arrows, if these are shot at random.

Tapirs are Tough

There is great rejoicing in the village today. The hunters have killed a tapir and there is fresh meat for everybody. Dona Eva is really glad that we have a pressure cooker, for tapir-meat is tough, especially after it has been salted and dried into leather-like strips in the hot sun.

Alive, a tapir is a very tough looking animal. His head is big, hard and stream-lined, a wonderful provision for life in the jungle. A cow has a big, hard head too, but she would have a bad time if she had to exchange her field for a tapir's forest. With those long horns she would get entangled in the undergrowth, and the loose skin about her throat would be torn by the thorns. The tapir's stream-lined head can crash through the densest thicket.

His skin too is thick and tough and even arrows do not always pierce him. His legs are short and powerful, hoofed and very sure-footed. His short trunk is just big enough to cover his mouth. He uses it to eat and communicate with other tapirs. The trunk is also sensitive to smells. The tapir can find out a lot of information about his surroundings by just sniffing with his trunk. When in danger, a tapir makes for the river at a speed which is truly amazing for one so heavy. Under water his legs go very fast and he swims like an otter. His feet have such a good grip that he can even walk underwater along the river bottom. His hoofed feet take him up the steepest, muddiest bank to safety.

Well, today the Kayapo hunters have killed a tapir! Perhaps you wonder how they do it with him being so well defended, so careful and quick. How do they get him with such primitive weapons as bow and arrows? The answer is that the Kayapos are cunning and patient, as well as being good marksmen.

They know all about the tapir. They have him all weighed up long before he is dead or even before the hunt begins. They know, for instance, that for an animal, he has some remarkably settled habits. He will stay quite a while in one locality. He likes to take a long, cool bath in the same place and at the same time each day. When he goes to bathe, he goes the same way, along the same trail. Unlike the monkey and the peccary, the tapir is usually on his own. If there is no danger about, he will sometimes raise his trunk and whistle, hoping that another lonely tapir will reply. How excited he gets when his call brings an answer!

Hunters know that tapirs like salt. Even though a tapir may never have tasted it before, he will linger to lick the ground if his trail has been salted.

Most important of all, is the knowledge that he has a weak spot, a chink in his armour. For all the strong limbs, the thick skin and the hard head, the Tapir has a big, open and undefended ear! Shoot an arrow or even a charge or buck-shot at random, and they will hurt no more that so many pin-pricks, but if one arrow or one bullet can get into that ear, down he will go!

So the wily hunters get to work. If they have salt, they will salt his trail. They will try him with a friendly call. They can imitate his whistle to perfection, calling to attract his attention or in answer to his own efforts to find a mate. Slowly, patiently, they lure him into range, and manoeuvre him into turning that open ear towards the bow and arrow prepared for his undoing.

Then one shot, and the tough tapir is laid low, an easy victim, provided the hunter has patience and know-how.

When the Lord Jesus called His first disciples, He said that He would make them 'fishers of men', to catch them for Him, not for their destruction but for their salvation.

Here in the Brazilian jungle, we both 'fish' and 'hunt' men for Jesus. It is the call to all the Lord's disciples. People are 'caught' when His word gets into their hearts, and they too believe and follow.

In the Kayapo language, the word for 'ear' is 'the hole which leads to the heart'. Many people have ears which seem to be so connected-up that whatever goes in at one side goes out through the other! But the Kayapo are right. The ear is God's ordained way of reaching the heart.

'Faith cometh by hearing and hearing by the Word of God.' (Romans 10:17)

Men were never easily caught, but good fishermen and hunters are never easily discouraged. They know that behind many a tough look and hard exterior, there is often a lonely, needy heart just waiting to respond to the right approach.

The Lord Jesus did not only preach. We read that he went throughout every city and village 'preaching and showing' the glad tidings of the Kingdom of God! (Luke 8:1)

If, as we seek others for Jesus, they do not seem to want to be caught; if our witness, shot at random, seems ineffective, we may well try a little more 'showing', in the way of friendliness, helpfulness and love, in order to better obtain their 'ear', and to get God's word right into their hearts.

The only member of
the elephant family
native to the American
continent is the tapir.

Tip from an Elephant Tamer!

Every summer the Kayapo make new clearings in the forest, so as to have somewhere to plant their maize and manioc when the rains come. First, they cut down the underwood, then the trees, and everything is left to dry out in the hot sun. Then the clearings are fired. There is never any danger of accidental forest fires by the Amazon, for very few of the trees are resinous, and 'green' wood will not burn. Even after two months drying the flames sometimes burn the leaves and smaller branches without doing more than scorch the heavier timber. Then the Kayapo have a hard time, for they must clear the unburned tree-trunks by hand, chopping them up and piling them into heaps for re-burning.

In some old magazines we were showing them, the Kayapo were amazed to see pictures of elephants using their trunks to carry and stack huge logs.

'Why ever aren't there any elephants in our jungle!' they moaned.

There aren't. The only member of the elephant family native to the American continent is the tapir.

From what we have seen of him, he must be a very distant relative indeed, with little in common apart from that stub of a trunk of his. Knowing how destructive and dangerous elephants can be, I'm glad that the only ones in America are those in zoos and circuses. With no really big game about, no rhinos or hippos, no lions or tigers to make the Kayapo run for their lives, the Kayapo tribe are without rivals for the lordship of the jungle. Though their weapons are only bows and arrows, wooden clubs and lances tipped with jaguar-bone, they are quite without fear as they tread their forest trails.

But there are other dangers in the Brazilian jungle. It is a dangerous place no one will deny - not because of wild beasts, or reptiles, but because of wild men!

Sometimes, in the evening, from our own village we have seen smoke in the far, far distance. When night has fallen, a glow in the sky has told that the tribe calling itself 'The People with Shaved Heads' are near by. For years they have terrorized the region more than wild elephants or lions could ever do. It can be a worry for natives and missionaries alike that at any moment they may walk into an ambush or expect an attack on their homes?

How to tame these people is a real problem. Fighting against them would be one way. But it is not the missionary's way. There is another way. If you wanted to tame a wild elephant in Africa or Asia how would you go about it? In these countries well-trained elephants can be used as decoys, to lure their wild relatives to their master's corral where they are broken-in, and tamed so that their great strength and intelligence can be harnessed to useful ends.

Missionaries can use decoys too. The decoys the missionaries like to send out are those they know intimately. They too, must know the missionaries, who they are, what they have, what they do. They may carry simple gifts such as beads, matches or fishhooks. They may be dressed in clothes the missionaries have provided. When sick, they have proved the value of the missionaries' medicine. They may have a book they learned to read in the mission school. The best decoys are the people who have heard about Jesus and follow him like the missionaries who taught them. They sing the Jesus-songs, and walk the Jesus-way. Being such a decoy is a serious business. They must be brave as well as trustworthy.

How we have prayed for our Kayapo friends as they have left us and gone in the direction of those forest fires! How excited we have been when, maybe weeks afterwards, they have returned to us bringing other tribes people we have never seen before.

Our friends who have heard and believed in Christ are now bringing others to us who have never before heard of the God who loves them. God's 'tamed' people bring the wild people to him. In Asia the wild elephant is brought into the corral and is made tame. How much more wonderful and amazing it is to see a person brought from being God's enemy to being his friend.

Isn't that just how God works, the wild world over? Christians, Jesus-hearers, are His 'tamed' ones. We have a Lord and Master Who has dealt with our own wildness and waywardness. We find joy and satisfaction in His service. In 1 John 4:19 we read that "We love Him because He first loved us." Do you love Jesus? If you do then the most important job He has given you to do is to call others to him.

Of course, we are not expected to say to them: 'Look at me. I am better than you are'. We are to tell them what a wonderful Master we have, and seek to lead them to Him, not drive them. We cannot do the taming, nor does our Master expect us to try. Only His word and His power and His love can do that. Our job is to go out and bring them in for the Master's hand to touch and tame.

In India the unusual white elephant is worshipped by some people. But we know what a useless old thing a white elephant can be. Big, strong, pampered creature, eating its master's food at the rate of about 70 kilos or 150 pounds per day, yet doing nothing. Because of some imagined sacredness, it lives a boring, idle life. If you had to be an elephant, would you want to be a white one?

'Work for Jesus,
day by day,
Serve Him ever,
Falter never,
Christ obey!
Yield Him service,
loyal, true;
There's a work for Jesus
none but you can do!

In the rain the jungle frog is in his element. The more it rains, the happier he seems to be and he lets everybody know it. Day and night throughout the winter, the swamp echoes with a mighty chorus of croaking frogs!

Froggy Shows the Way

I've told this story before but there are so many lessons that we can learn - particularly from the peculiar little fellow that we bumped into in our house one day.

"Come quickly, and see this strange frog!" called Dona Eva, from her kitchen. I went, although I did not hurry. Frogs aren't that unusual in the rain forest and there are many different types. I always see unusual things in the Kayapo village, and unusual people too. But it really was a strange frog. It was jet black and unusually flat in its appearance... a bit like a pancake. Dona suggested that he had been crushed. What impressed me was that crushed or no, the frog's chin was up!

Left to himself, the frog hopped into the shadows behind the water-pot where it was not only dark, but cool. 'Let him stay', said Dona Eva, kindly. 'This is only the kitchen, and after all, even frogs have to live somewhere.'

After spawning and growing from a small black tadpole to the big frog it now was our frog had hopped across from a swamp on the outskirts of the village, where another million of its kind had spent the winter.

Winter is a dreary time for most jungle-dwellers. The Kayapo detest it. The tortoise is fortunate in that he can hibernate and only wake up when the sun shines again. The cheery cricket gets depressed and gives up chirping as soon as winter comes. Almost alone among jungle creatures, the frog is in his element. The more it rains, the happier he seems to be and he lets everybody know it. Day and night throughout the winter, the swamp has echoed with a mighty chorus of croaking frogs!

Curiously enough, they croak 'N-go n-go n-go', which is the Kayapo word for water.

When the rains finish, the swamps begin to dry up. All the frogs must scatter if they are to survive. So they make for the water-holes which do not disappear during the six months when rain is but a dream. Once installed, they resume their croaking, although it may only be on an evening when the heat of the day has passed.

Many and many a time when travelling through the forest, I have been grateful for the friendly, water-loving frogs. Dreadfully thirsty, with no sign of water anywhere, the guides have listened carefully until some lone frog's croaking has led us to a water hole. A dog barks when angry or excited. A cat mews when hungry or in pain. A rooster crows to tell the world what a fine fellow he is to get up so early in the morning. The frog croaks because he has found water, or because rain is coming, and he seems to want everybody to know! Yes, the poor, black, crushed-looking frog was quite at liberty to stay behind our water-pot.

However, later in the day, the frog was found in the bedroom! From time to time, the water-pot had to be taken down to the river to be refilled, and this, no doubt, had brought him undesired publicity. Hence his desire to explore the bedroom. This seemed to be imposing on our good nature, and picking up a broom, I took action and our frog was most unceremoniously brushed back into the kitchen. As he hopped back into his old corner, the poor fellow looked flatter and more sat-on than ever.

When night fell, I lit the pressure lamp and sat down to a supper of boiled fish, very grateful for a good light so that I could pick out the bones. But would you believe it, there was that frog again, his chin higher than ever as he hopped round the inside walls of the dining room!

What was he doing? Why, mopping up mosquitoes! Terrible things, those mosquitoes. Not content to bite and fill up with blood, they pass on malaria to their victims. During the day time, and after they are well fed at night, they hide in chinks in the mud walls. But there was the frog, rooting them out with his long tongue. If he saw one out of range, he would jump up and get it while air-borne.

'Good old fellow!' I muttered. 'There you go, sat on and kicked out yet quite undismayed and with no ill-feeling at all, getting on with the good work while the rest of the world takes it easy!' How often Dona Eva and I have felt sat-on and crushed as we have tried to say something or do something for God! Did you ever feel that way, your efforts quite unappreciated, never mind achieving the results you sought?

Listen! If a puny creature like a frog can refuse to be discouraged, if he can keep his chin up in the face of opposition and not let it interfere with his programme of doing good, if he can be at his best when the weather

is at its worst, and never tire of saying 'Water, water, water!', then surely we can take courage. The Lord Jesus is the living water so ready and able to satisfy every thirsty soul which comes to Him. We must tell the world!

There was a sudden scampering of beetles, as big as mice, and overhead the chirping and fluttering of bats which had been having the time of their lives in the big, dark, empty house.

The Closed House

Missionaries get holidays too you know. How good it is to get back to civilization after so long in the wilds! To see a postman again after living a month's journey from the nearest post-office! To breakfast on bread rolls and butter with as many cups of tea or coffee as you can drink! To sit at a table covered with a snowy-white cloth and hear the tinkle of dainty china instead of the clatter of tins and enamel plates! It's good to spend time in one of the more cosmopolitan areas of Brazil - it's a break from the harshness of jungle life and we can catch up with some of our other Brazilian friends.

The front door is wide-open, Brazilian fashion, all day long. The neighbours come along to bid us welcome. As they sit and drink very black coffee from the tiniest of cups, their eyes look around with satisfaction and they tell us how glad they are to see the house open and happy again, after being locked-up, silent and sad, for so long.

Yes, the house was just that, when we arrived. Imagine the home-coming. I unlocked the outside gate. It creaked on its hinges and positively groaned for the oil-can. The backyard was overgrown with weeds such as only the tropics can produce. The cobbles were slippery with moss and slime. As each inside door was opened, we were greeted with the smell or mildew and the feel of dampness.

In some rooms there was a sudden scampering of beetles as big as mice, and overhead the chirping and fluttering of bats which had been having the time of their lives in the big, dark, empty house.

Then we inspected the baggage and home-made furniture. "Have the white-ants been busy? Any damage through the rain dripping from a leaky roof? Anything stolen?" What exclamations of relief as everything was found more or less intact!

Finally, there was the spring-cleaning of every nook and cranny in the house, with Dona Eva blithely swinging her broom and me following with bucket and shovel. As we worked together, I told her of a previous home-coming.

'It was one Sunday, and I had barely time to sweep out the front room before the people began to arrive for the evening service.

'During the first hymn, there was sudden cry of "Cobra!" and the singing had to stop while one of the few Kayapo present arrowed a snake which was wriggling in and out of the straw thatch. Throwing the dead snake behind the preacher's table, the man went back to his place and the singing continued.

'Before many minutes had passed, the same cry went up again, and once more we had to wait while a snake was despatched. Nor was that the end. That night, no less than five snakes were killed in that old straw roof!

'How glad I was when morning came, and I was able to open all the doors and windows and let in the fresh air and God's lovely clean sunshine.

'Ever since that little experience, I've been very careful when opening doors which have been closed for a long while. I know what to expect, and I usually have a big stick handy!'

Dona Eva was thinking of a picture she had seen of the Lord Jesus standing outside a closed door, not in the tropics, but somewhere nearer home. Though it looks like the door of a house, it is really the door of a heart. In the hand of Jesus, who is knocking, is not a stick but a lantern.

Closed houses where you live probably do not harbour the horrid things we find in the dark places of Brazil, but closed hearts are the same everywhere. They harbour secrets and sins only known to their owners and to the One who stands at the heart's door. When the Pharisees wanted to know how His disciples could eat without washing their hands, Jesus said to them: 'Not that which goeth into the mouth defileth a man, but that which cometh out of the mouth... those things which proceed out of the mouth come from the heart, and they defile the man. For out of the heart proceed evil thoughts.... thefts... false witness... blasphemies. These are the things which defile.' (Matthew 15:11,19,20)

'Behold I stand at the door, and knock, if any man hear My voice and open the door, I will come in to Him.' (Rev. 3:20)

He seeks admission because He wants to put things right, to make our hearts His home, clean, safe and happy.

The bees live in hollow trees, and go in and out through a tiny hole in the trunk. The kinkajou is expert at finding and exploring these holes. Being able to hang by his tail, both hands are left free for the job. In goes a hand, and out comes the honey!

What Kinkajou can do!

I was on furlough. The Amazon forest was far away and instead of treading a narrow trail, I was walking along a crowded footpath in my home town on the banks of the river Mersey.

Suddenly I stopped and looked up at a most fascinating face which seemed to be smiling down at me from one of the large advertising hoardings. It was the cute furry little South American kinkajou. Enjoying all the limelight in a great big refreshments advertisement in England.

The large advertisement was for alcohol and kinkajou was perched there with a glass of it between his two paws. It was rather strange for me to see him sitting there - I was so used to seeing him in his natural habitat in Brazil - but here he was in the middle of Liverpool.

'Well, well!' I muttered. 'However have you managed it kinkajou? All the way from the native Central and South American jungle to England! And enjoying all the limelight in that advertisement too. A few months advertising has made you as well known as the elephant and camel.' I read the advertising slogan, 'Just think what kinkajou can do.'

How cute he looked, with those big eyes and that brown fur coat. How many boys and girls must have admired him and wished that they could have him for a pet! But I felt uneasy as I saw him there beside a glass of beer - it wasn't right. It wasn't where he was supposed to be. He should have been at home in Brazil. And I knew the other side of kinkajou - on the advertisement he looks cute - but in his home country of Brazil there is another side to his nature.

In Brazil kinkajou is just one of his many native names. Some Kayapo call him krokrok. Others call him the equivalent of honey-tooth. Of course, there is no beer for him in the jungle, but there is plenty of wild honey and he knows exactly where to look for it.

The bees live in hollow trees, and go in and out through a tiny hole in the trunk. The kinkajou is expert at finding and exploring these holes. Being able to hang by his tail, both hands are left free for the job. In goes a hand, and out comes the honey!

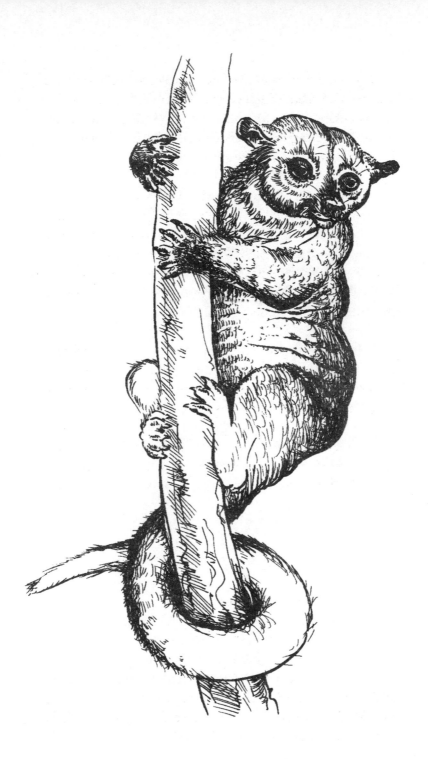

Now for all my many years in South America, I've never once seen a kinkajou at work. The Kayapo don't see him either, nor would you, even though you should live there. That is because the kinkajou is nocturnal. He only goes out at night. If you really wanted to see him at work, you might have to spend many nights in the tree tops, waiting for him, with a flash light. Should you wish to take his picture, you would need a flash camera. Though he seems to enjoy our sunshine, and the publicity of our advertisements, he is much more at home in the dark. In the forest where he belongs, he slinks about at night like the rats, the mosquitoes and vampire bats.

In the advertisement he is shown as having a very sweet tooth - it's supposed to be a joke - because the beer he is advertising is supposed to be sweet. In the jungle, that sweet tooth is a sharp one. His interest in hollow trees is not limited to the bees and the honey they make. There are birds which nest in the same kind of place, to be safe from hawks. But they are never safe from innocent looking kinkajou! The two clever hands which can be trained to lift a glass of beer or extract a piece of luscious honeycomb, can pluck living birds from their nests and tear them wing from wing! The kinkajou is not only nocturnal - he's carnivorous. He likes honey, but he likes meat, too, warm red meat just as does the jaguar and the hawk.

I'm no admirer of the kinkajou. Do you remember how I mentioned that he has another side to his nature? When I saw him smiling down from the hoardings, with those two roguish eyes, two pixy ears and two cute hands, I wanted to say to him: 'Yes, and you also have two faces! One here for people to see and admire, another for your victims. One face for the advertisement, quite a different one for your home. You two-faced double-dealer!'

Among those who do not know him properly, the kinkajou may make a good impression. Many will believe what the advert says and think that alcohol is good for them. But those who know about the two faces will suspect that there is something wrong here.

The kinkajou is the best illustration of the drink business that the artist could have painted! Just like kinkajou, strong drink has two faces, one glamorous and bright, the other selfish and heartless. On the posters, it sparkles. On the streets, it spoils. One face for the advertisement, another for the home, just like kinkajou!'

For an advertisement to convince, it must ring true. What is blazoned in big letters and bright colours on the posters, must be demonstrated in real life. Christians must also show God's power in their life. They can't say one thing and behave in another. When you say that you believe in Jesus Christ your life must show this to be true in the way you speak and act. You must be like Jesus Christ, the one you say that you love, follow and obey.

Men need our testimony, Christ commands it. We are to be living advertisements of His love, purity and power. But if the world is to believe us, our witness must pass the sincerity test.

'Be like Jesus, this my song,
In the home and in the throng,
Be like Jesus, all day long,
I would be like Jesus!'

Amazon Quiz

1   What creature is a dynamo, battery and discharge coil?

2   How many volts does it produce?

3   Who said, 'All power is given unto me in heaven and in earth'?

4   How many types of butterfly live in the Brazilian Jungle?

5   In the story how long was the white mayfly's life cycle?

6   Why did Jesus come to earth?

7   What animal's legs are fitted with grips like the teeth of a saw?

8   The grasshopper is a member of what insect family?

9   Who has the words of eternal life?

10   Who is 'Lion of the earth' but isn't fierce?

11   What does he use as a hook when climbing trees?

12 Which disciple was a turn-coat?

13 How heavy is an emu's egg?

14 What does an ostrich eat?

15 What is unusual about an ostrich's wings?

16 Is an ostrich fast or slow?

17 In what book of the Bible do we read 'Let us run with patience the race set before us. Looking unto Jesus...' ?

18 Which animal has a shell that matches the dead leaves of the rainforest?

19 Who lived for 969 years before he died?

20 Where do female tortoises lay eggs?

21 What does the word witness mean?

22 What animal can walk under water?

23 What do the hunters use to catch a Tapir?

24 What is 'The hole that leads to the heart'?

25 Faith comes by hearing and hearing comes from something else. What is that?

26 What two crops do the Amazon Indians grow?

27 What do Amazon Indians hunt with?

28 In 1 John 4:19 it talks about someone who loves us. Who is this?

29 What do frogs do during the Amazonian winter?

30 What does a frog like to eat?

31 What disease is spread by mosquitos?

32 Who is the living water who satisfys thirsty souls?

33 What dangerous snake did the missionaries tackle?

34 Who can change our sinful hearts?

35 What is the other name for a krokrok?

36 How does it get its name honey-tooth?

37 What other things does it eat?

38 If you are a Christian who must you behave like and remind people of?

Answers

1	Electric Eel	20	In the Sand
2	500	21	Messenger
3	Jesus Christ	22	Tapir
4	30,000	23	Salt
5	4 hours	24	Ear
6	To save us from our sins	25	Word of God
7	Grasshopper	26	Maize/Manioc
8	Locust	27	Bow and Arrows
9	Jesus Christ	28	Jesus/God
10	Chameleon	29	Croak
11	His tail	30	Mosquitos
12	Judus	31	Malaria
13	Just under half a kilo or over a pound	32	Jesus Christ
		33	Cobra
14	Anything	34	Jesus Christ
15	They aren't used for flying	35	Kinkajou
16	Fast	36	It raids Bee Hives
17	Hebrews	37	Birds/meat
18	Tortoise or Turtle	38	Jesus Christ.
19	Methuselah		

Rainforest Adventures
by Horace Banner

If you have enjoyed this book then look out for the other title in this series: Rainforest Adventures.

The Amazon Rainforest is the oldest and largest rain forest in the world. Covering a huge area of South America it has the most varied plant and animal habitat on the planet. Read this book and you will join an expedition into the heart of the rain forest.

Discover the tree Frog's nest, the chamelon who can change it's colour and the very hungry piranha fish. Even the possum can teach a lesson about speaking out for Jesus Christ and the parasol ant can show us how to keep going and not give up. Then there's the brightly coloured toucan whose call reminds us that with God we can do anything. Discover what its like to actually live in the Rain forest. Join in the adventures and experience the exciting and dangerous life of a pioneer missionary in South America.

ISBN: 1-85792-627-7

LIGHT
KEEPERS

Ten Boys who changed the World

Would you like to change your world? These ten boys grew up to do just that:

Billy Graham, Brother Andrew, John Newton, George Muller, Nicky Cruz, William Carey, David Livingstone, Adoniram Judson, Eric Liddell, Luis Palau.

Find out how Eric won the race and honoured God; David became an explorer and explained the Bible; Nicky joined the gangs and then the church; Andrew smuggled Bibles into Russian and brought hope to thousands and John captured slaves but God used him to set them free.

Find out what God wants you to do!

ISBN: 1-85792-579-3

Ten Girls who changed the World

Would you like to change your world? These ten girls grew up to do just that:

Isobel Kuhn, Elizabeth Fry, Amy Carmichael, Gladys Aylward, Mary Slessor, Catherine Booth, Jackie Pullinger, Evelyn Brand, Joni Eareckson Tada, Corrie Ten Boom.

Find out how Corrie saved lives and loved Jesus in World War II; Mary saved babies in Africa and fought sin; Gladys rescued 100 children and trusted God; Joni survived a crippling accident and still thanked Jesus; Amy rescued orphans and never gave up; Isobel taught the Lisu about Christ and followed him; Evelyn obeyed God in India and taught others too; Jackie showed love in awful conditions in Hong Kong; Elizabeth showed compassion and helped prisoners; and Catherine rolled up her sleeves and helped the homeless!

Find out what God wants you to do!

ISBN: 1-85792-649-8

CHRISTIAN FOCUS

Good books with the real message of hope!

Christian Focus Publications publishes biblically-accurate books for adults and children.

If you are looking for quality Bible teaching for children then we have a wide and excellent range of Bible story books - from board books to teenage fiction, we have it covered.

You can also try our new Bible teaching Syllabus for 3-9 year olds and teaching materials for pre-school children.

These children's books are bright, fun and full of biblical truth, an ideal way to help children discover Jesus Christ for themselves. Our aim is to help children find out about God and get them enthusiastic about reading the Bible, now and later in their lives.

**Find us at our web page:
www.christianfocus.com**